ANDREA CAPPELLARI

FIRST BOOK
OF CLASSICAL TRUMPET

TRUMPET

To access companion recorded accompaniments
online, visit:
www.halleonard.com/mylibrary
Enter Code
3820-0202-3820-3381

ISBN 978-1-5400-5463-0

RICORDI

EXCLUSIVELY DISTRIBUTED BY

Visit Hal Leonard Online at
www.halleonard.com

Contact us:
Hal Leonard
7777 West Bluemound Road
Milwaukee, WI 53213
Email: info@halleonard.com

In Europe, contact:
Hal Leonard Europe Limited
42 Wigmore Street
Marylebone, London, W1U 2RN
Email: info@halleonardeurope.com

In Australia, contact:
Hal Leonard Australia Pty. Ltd.
4 Lentara Court
Cheltenham, Victoria, 3192 Australia
Email: info@halleonard.com.au

Andrea Cappellari holds degrees in choral music and choral conducting, music education, and percussion instruments from the Giuseppe Verdi Conservatory in Milan. He is a lecturer at the Giacomo Puccini Higher Institute of Music Studies in Gallarate, Varese, Italy, and at the Candiani-Bausch High School of the Arts in Busto Arsizio, Varese, Italy. He teaches training and continuing education courses for teachers and courses in rhythm and ensemble music in French-speaking Switzerland. He is a director of choral and instrumental ensembles, and author of numerous educational publications and collections of children's songs.

In memory of my beloved mother Wanda.

Thanks to Simone Ronzoni
Cover Art by Giuseppe Spada

INTRODUCTION

Inside the training course for the instrumentalist, *First Book of Classical Trumpet* proposes an invaluable collection of 100 melodies by classical composers arranged and ordered by progressive difficulty.

The collection allows the beginning instrumentalist to discover, through a practical approach, the repertoire of the great classical tradition.

The trumpet is a very special instrument, with a sound able to express memories and sensations belonging to the military and heroic life of our past.

Sergio Gianzini
director at the Higher Institute of Musical Studies "Giacomo Puccini" in Gallarate, Italy

CONTENTS

MELODIES INDEXED BY COMPOSER

1 **Melodies of 3 Notes/Rhythmic Values:**

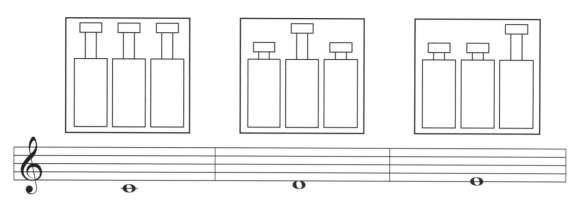

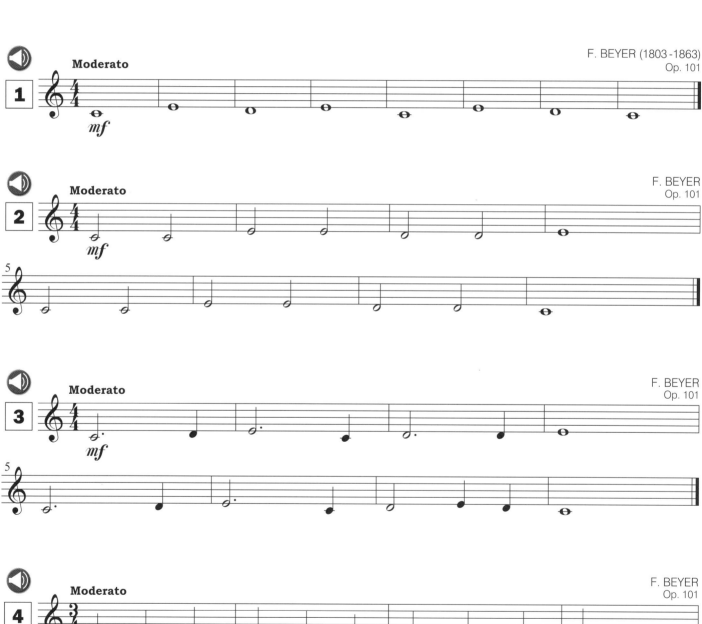

2 Melodies of 4 Notes/Rhythmic Values: 𝅝 𝅗𝅥. 𝅗𝅥 ♩

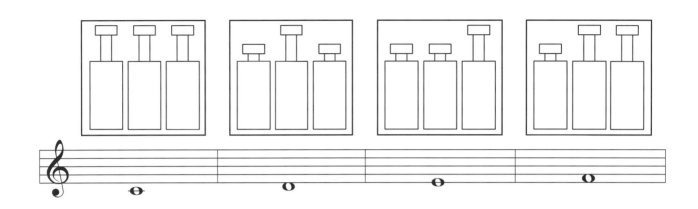

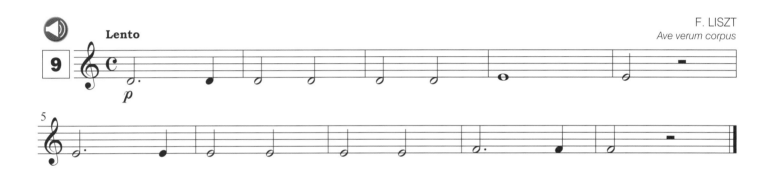

F. LISZT
Ave verum corpus

F. BEYER
Op. 101

F. BEYER
Op. 101

3 Melodies of 5 Notes/Rhythmic Values: o d. d ♩

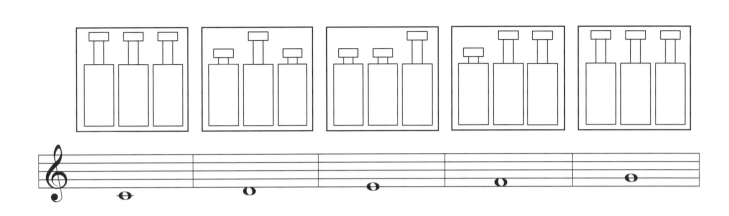

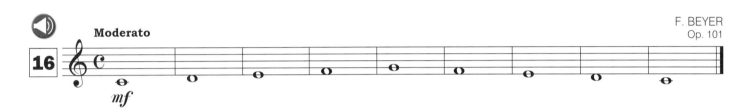

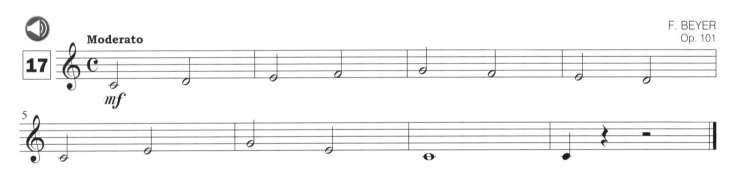

Preparatory Exercises

C. CZERNY (1791-1857)
Op. 777

F. BEYER
Op. 101

5 Melodies of 6 Notes/Rhythmic Values: from 𝅝 to ♪

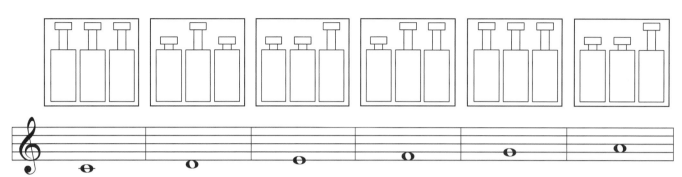

6 Melodies of 5 Notes/Rhythmic Values: from 𝅗𝅥. to ♪

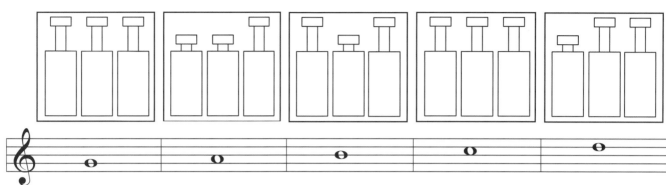

7 C-Major Scale

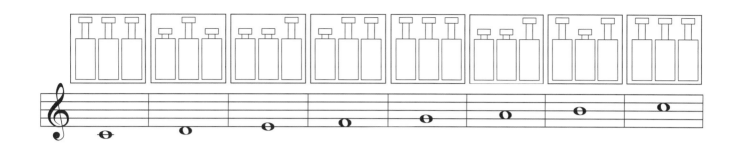

E. GRANADOS (1867-1916)
Waltz

41 **Melodioso**

A. DVOŘÁK (1841-1904)
Slavonic Dance Op. 46 n. 1

42 **Presto**

M.A. CHARPENTIER
Vous qui désirez sans fin

43 **Non troppo veloce**

W.A. MOZART
Deutsche Tänze - Serie 11 n. 13

N. PORPORA
Concerto IV

B. GALUPPI (1706-1785)
Kyrie (Missa in Do)

B. GALUPPI
Sanctus (Missa in Do)

Melodies of 5 Notes/Rhythmic Values: from 𝅝 to ♪

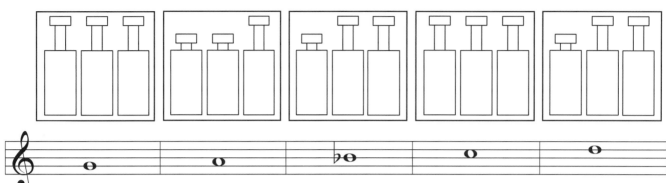

F. BEYER
Op. 101

53 Allegretto

p

Fine

D.C. al Fine

F. BEYER
Op. 101

54 Andante

mf

[Moderato]

D. MANZOLO (17th century)

55

p

FIRST BOOK OF CLASSICAL TRUMPET

37 **Un poco animato** — A. SCHMOLL *Petit Étude*

38 **Assai vivo** — A. SCHMOLL *Petit Étude*

39 **[Allegretto]** — M. CORRETTE (1707-1795) *Menuet allemand*

40 **Lento** — M.A. CHARPENTIER (1634-1704) *Domine Deus (Messe de minuit)*

41 **Melodioso** — E. GRANADOS (1867-1916) *Waltz*

42 **Presto** — A. DVOŘÁK (1841-1904) *Slavonic Dance* Op. 46 n. 1

D. BUXTEHUDE (1637-1707) Sinfonia: *Du Friedefürst*

99   Lento   1.   A. SCHMOLL *En prière*

100   Andantino   F. BURGMÜLLER (1806-1874) *Ave Maria*

G. GASTOLDI (1555-1622)
La cortigiana

A. FOOTE (1853-1937)
A little Waltz

A. DIABELLI (1781-1858)
Alla turca

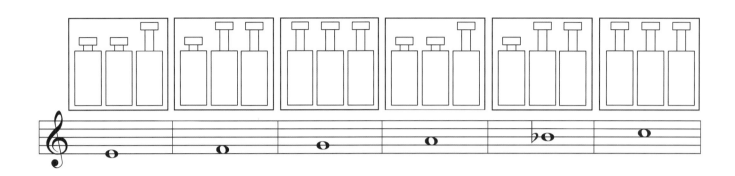

D. BUXTEHUDE (1637-1707)
Sinfonia: Du Friedefürst

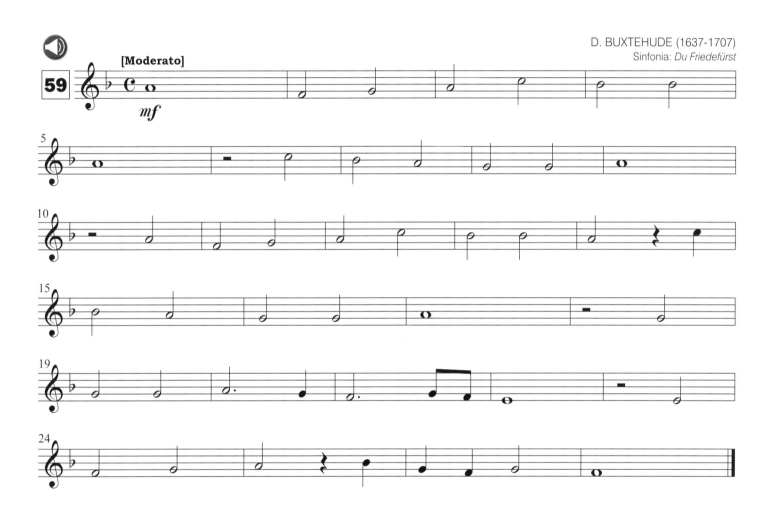

59 [Moderato]

P.B. GRUBER (1759-1796)
Ave Regina coelorum

60 Andante

10 Melodies of 4 Notes/Rhythmic Values: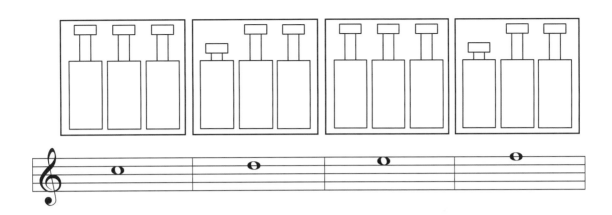

K.M. KUNZ (1812-1875)
Canons Op. 14

61

K.M. KUNZ
Canons Op. 14

62

K.M. KUNZ
Canons Op. 14

63

11 Melodies of 3 Notes/Rhythmic Values: 𝅝 𝅗𝅥 𝅘𝅥

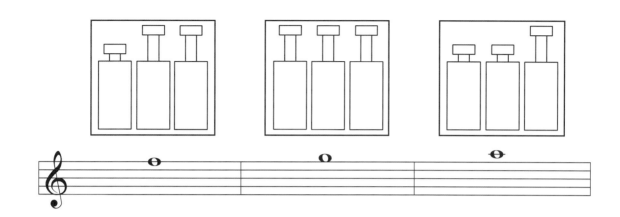

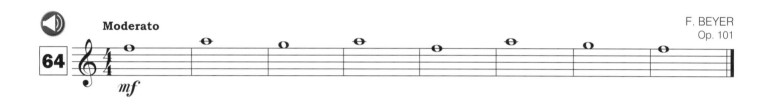

F. BEYER
Op. 101

64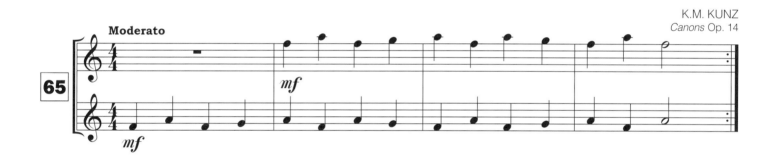

K.M. KUNZ
Canons Op. 14

65

K.M. KUNZ
Canons Op. 14

66

12 F-Major Scale

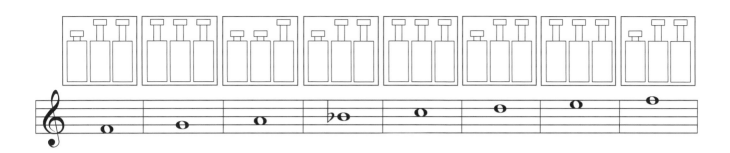

J. ROSENMÜLLER (1619-1684)
Meine Seele harret auf Gott

67 Presto

L.E. GEBHARDI (1787-1862)
2-Part canon

68 Moderato

M. HAYDN
Wie trostreich

69 Moderato

13 Melodies of 5 Notes/Rhythmic Values: from 𝅝 to ♪

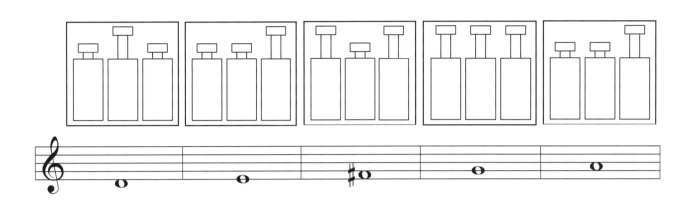

F. BEYER
Op. 101

77 Moderato
mf

Anonymous (18th century)
Magnificat

78 [Andante]
mf

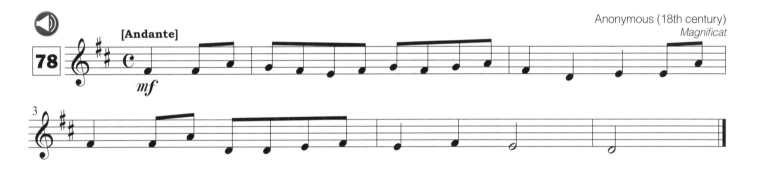

W.A. MOZART
Minuetto (Symphony n. 35)

79 [Andante]
p

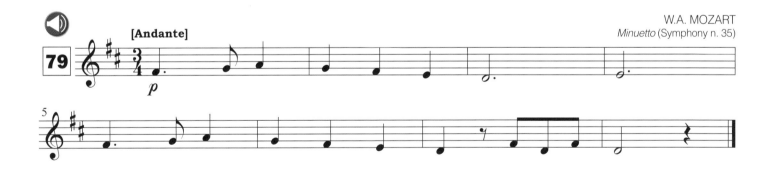

C. CZERNY
Op. 777

80 Allegro
p

14 Melodies of 6 Notes/Rhythmic Values: from 𝅝 to ♪

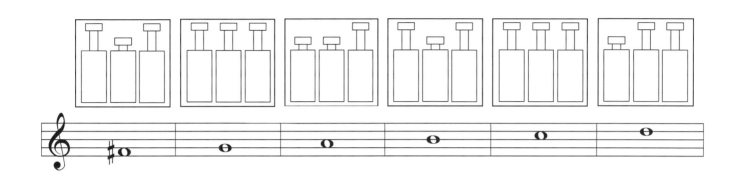

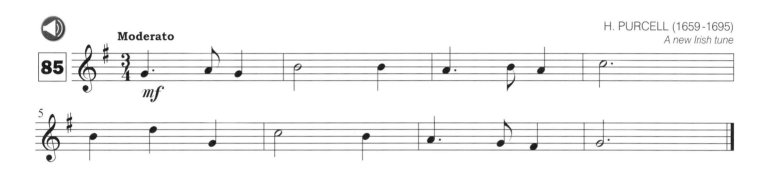

H. PURCELL (1659-1695)
A new Irish tune

Moderato

85 *mf*

A. FOOTE
Reverie

Andante

86 *p*

W.A. MOZART
Deutsche Tänze - Serie 11 n. 13

[Allegro]

87 *mf*

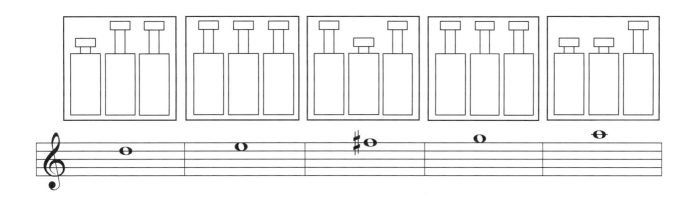

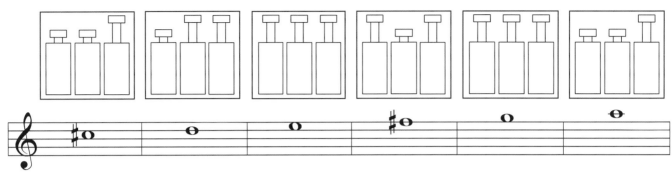

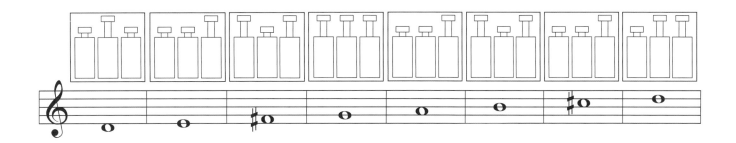

G. LANGE (1830-1889)
Arietta - Sonatina Op. 114 n. 4

93 Andantino
mf

F. SCHUBERT (1797-1828)
Tänze Serie 12 n. 1

94 Moderato
p

I. PLEYEL
Rondò - Sonatina n.1

95 Moderato
mf

18 G-Major Scale

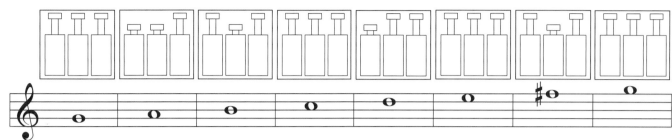

Moderato

L.E. GEBHARDI
Morgengesang

96

mf

5

[Andante]

L.E. GEBHARDI
Wasserlied

97

mf

6

12

L.E. GEBHARDI
Der Sommerabend

98

A. SCHMOLL
En prière

99

F. BURGMÜLLER (1806-1874)
Ave Maria

100

FINGERING CHART

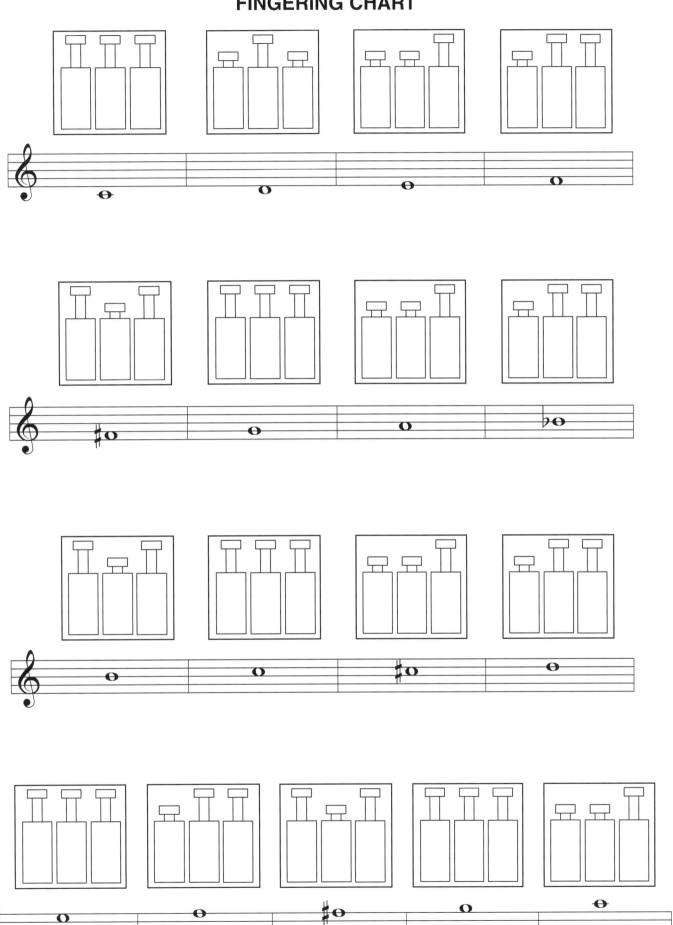

GLOSSARY

A tempo giusto	*In strict tempo*
Adagio religioso	*Slow, devotional*
Allegretto	*Fairly quick*
Allegro	*Fast*
Allegro moderato	*Moderately fast*
Andante	*Walking tempo*
Andante con moto	*Walking tempo with motion*
Andante moderato	*Moderate walking tempo*
Andante non troppo	*Walking tempo not too much*
Andantino	*Close to walking tempo*
Animato	*Animatedly*
Assai vivo	*Very lively*
Brillante e vivace	*Brilliant and lively*
Comodo	*Comfortably*
Con moto	*With motion*
Larghetto	*A little broad*
Largo	*Broad*
Lento	*Slow*
Maestoso ma non lento	*Majestic but not slow*
Melodioso	*Singing*
Menuetto grazioso	*Graceful minuet*
Moderato	*Moderately*
Molto allegro	Very quick
Non troppo veloce	*Not too rapidly*
Presto	*Very fast*
Un poco animato	*A little animated*
Vivace	*Lively*